A Gift For:

_____

From:

_____

Adapted from the book *The Middle Place* by Kelly Corrigan.
Copyright © 2008 Kelly Corrigan.
Adaptation copyright © 2012 Kelly Corrigan.
This special gift edition published in 2012 by arrangement with Voice,
an imprint of Hyperion, exclusively for Hallmark Cards, Inc.

Published by Hallmark Gift Books,
a division of Hallmark Cards, Inc.,
Kansas City, MO 64141
Visit us on the Web at www.Hallmark.com.

Editor: Jared Smith
Art Director: Kevin Swanson
Designer: Rob Latimer
Production Designer: Bryan Ring
ISBN: 978-1-59530-496-4
BOK4149

Printed and bound in China
JAN12

We Will
TRANSCEND

The Power of Women's Friendship

Kelly Corrigan

Hallmark
GIFT BOOKS

voice

an imprint of Hyperion

I had one of those

milestone birthdays

a few months back.

After the party got going,

I tried to make a toast—

something about friendship,

something about my mother and her friends

who call themselves "The Pigeons"

(a twist on The Hens)—

but it was rowdy

and my friend Shannon

was heckling me,

so I kept it short. Anyway,

this is what I wanted to say:

There were once a dozen Pigeons,

but in the past few years,

they lost two

of the greats—

Robin Burch and

Mary Maroney—

to cancer.

On the Pigeons go, though,

like women do,

limping one minute,

carrying someone the next.

They started in the '60s,

in suburban Philadelphia,

with bridge and tennis

and chardonnay—okay, vodka—

and over time became something

like a dedicated fleet,

armed ships sailing together,

weather be damned.

For me and women
of my generation,
it started with playdates,
cutting carbs, and meeting
on Monday mornings
in workout clothes

to do awkward moves

with large colorful balls.

And I can see

exactly where it's heading.

We'll confer about

jog bras and contractors

and pediatricians.

We'll gossip about
babysitters, teachers,
and in-laws.

We'll speculate about

who's had a shot of Botox,

who cheats on their taxes,

who cleans until midnight.

We'll celebrate

each other's achievements:

opening an exercise studio,

a corner store,

a jewelry business.

We'll celebrate

our kids' achievements:

making the traveling team,

singing in the choir,

learning to knit

or speak French

or play the flute.

We'll borrow eggs, earrings,

extra chairs. We'll throw

birthday parties for each other

and stain the rugs

and shatter the wineglasses

and mark up new counters

with the odd slice of lemon.

We'll worry about

who seems down,

who looks tired,

who's drinking more and more.

We'll say things

we'll wish we hadn't

and have to find a way

to regain each other's trust.

Things will break,

they always do.

Many will be fixed.

We'll fret

over our children:

too shy,

too angry,

too needy.

We'll brainstorm

ways to help them

become more resilient,

patient,

lighthearted.

We'll protect them—fiercely—

pulling little bodies

from the deep end,

double-latching windows,

withholding car keys.

We'll bury

our mothers and our fathers—

shuttling our children off for sleepovers,

jumping on red-eyes,

telling each other stories

that hurt to hear,

about gasping, agonal breaths,

hospice nurses, scars

and bruises and scabs,

and how skin papers

shortly after a person passes.

We will nod in agreement

that it is as much an honor

to witness a person

leave this world

as it is

to watch a person

come into it.

We'll admire each other

for a fine crème brûlée,

a promotion,

a finished marathon.

We'll commiserate about

commutes, layoffs,

mortgage rates,

the digital divide.

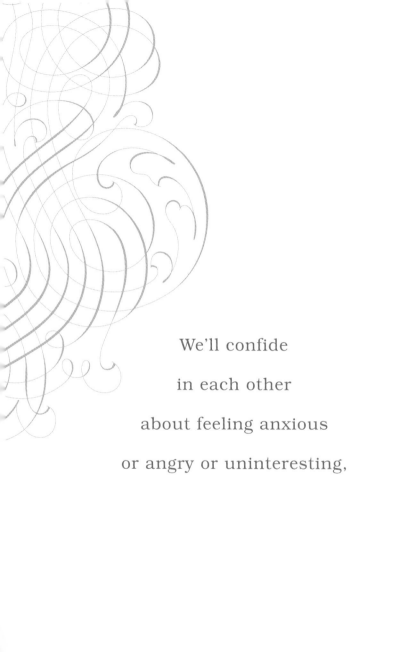

We'll confide

in each other

about feeling anxious

or angry or uninteresting,

or how many pieces

of Halloween candy

we accidentally ate

from our kids' bags.

We'll confess

that we text while driving,

or that we should be

having more sex,

or that we yell at our kids

every day.

We'll admit that

we believe in God,

Jesus Christ,

Heaven and Hell—

or that we don't.

People will drift in and out.

Book clubs will swell and thin.

We'll write someone off,

and they'll reemerge later

and we'll remember

both why we love them

and why we let them slip away,

but we'll be softer

and we'll want them back.

We'll give up

things together—

caffeine,

Tylenol PM,

catalogs,

social smoking.

We'll take up things too—

morning walks,

hybrids,

organic dairy,

saying grace.

We'll persuade each other to bake,

sell, fold, stuff, paint,

and write checks for our

favorite non-profits.

We'll diagnose each other's

brown lawns, torn muscles,

basement odors.

We'll check each other's

heads for lice,

and examine new bumps

and moles, and listen

to a list of symptoms.

We'll teach each other

how to set a ring tone,

make a slide show,

download a movie.

We will call

and say

"I heard the news"

and whatever the news is,

we will come running,

probably with food.

We'll insist

on second opinions,

lots of rest,

and the best surgeon.

We will face

diseases,

many kinds,

and will—temporarily—

lose our hair,

our figures,

and our minds.

Eventually, someone who's

not supposed to die will—

maybe one of us,

maybe a husband,

God forbid a child—

and all this celebrating

and sharing and confessing

will make certain

essential comforts possible.

We'll rally around

and hold each other up,

and it won't be nearly enough

but it will help the time pass

just a hair faster

than it would have otherwise.

We will wait

patiently and lovingly

for that first laugh

after the loss.

When it comes,

and it will come,

we will cry as we howl,

as we clutch, as we circle.

We will transcend, ladies.

Because we did all this,

in that worst moment,

we will transcend.

If you have enjoyed this book
or it has touched your life in some way,
we would love to hear from you.

Please send your comments to:
Hallmark Book Feedback
P.O. Box 419034
Mail Drop 215
Kansas City, MO 64141

Or e-mail us at:
booknotes@hallmark.com